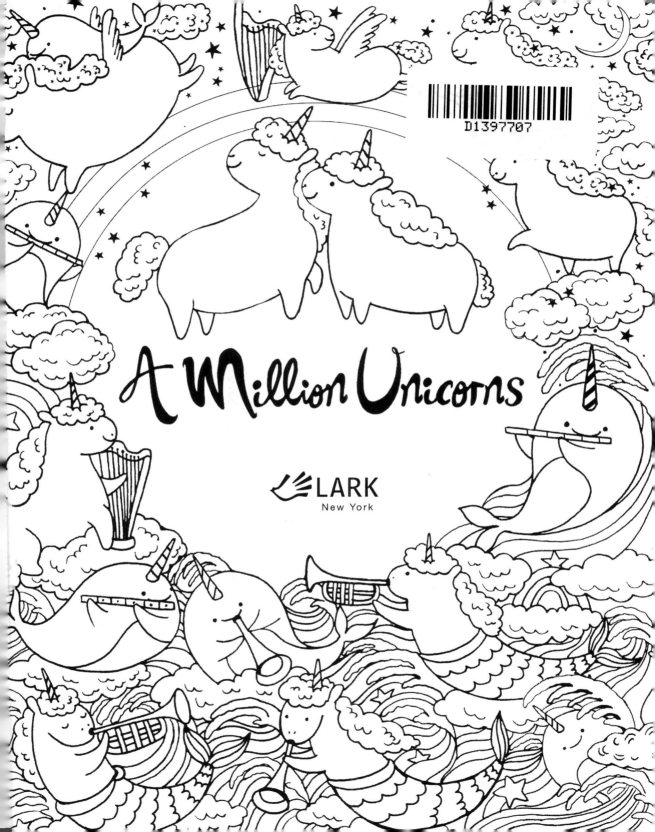

A Million Unicorns

LARK
New York

LARK

New York

An Imprint of Sterling Publishing Co., Inc.
1166 Avenue of the Americas
New York, NY 10036

First published in the United Kingdom in 2019 by Michael O'Mara Books Ltd.

ISBN 978-1-4547-1111-7

Distributed in Canada by Sterling Publishing Co., Inc.
c/o Canadian Manda Group, 664 Annette Street
Toronto, Ontario M6S 2C8, Canada

For information about custom editions, special sales, and premium and corporate purchases,
please contact Sterling Special Sales at 800-805-5489 or specialsales@sterlingpublishing.com.

Manufactured in Canada

4 6 8 10 9 7 5 3

sterlingpublishing.com/larkcrafts

Illustrated by

Lulu Mayo

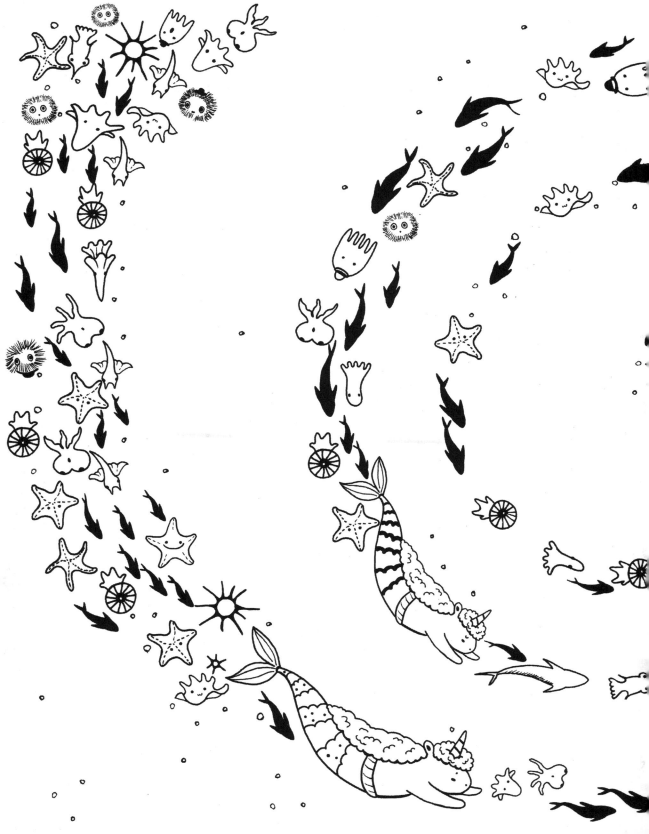